First published in Great Britain in 1998
by Walker Books Ltd. London

© 1998 Catherine and Laurence Anholt

Printed in Belgium

ISBN 1-58048-025-X

Catherine and Laurence Anholt's
BiG BooK of FAMiLiES

Baby's First Book Club®

Families together ...

Families laughing,

families learning,

families loving,

Families sharing,

families shouting,

families shoving,

Families talking,

families teasing,

families tugging,

Families helping,

families hoping,

families hugging.

Where do families live?

Up in cities, down on farms,
In bungalows, basements, buses, barns,
In cottages, castles, caravans, caves,
Blown by the winds, rocked by the waves.

In busy harbors, perched on sticks,
In igloos of ice and towers of bricks,
On mountains, islands, snow, and sand,
Families together in every land.

My sister lives in Singapore,

Cousin Kate's in Cork,

My auntie lives in Ecuador,

Her nephew's in New York.

Madeline's in Manchester,

Michael's in Milan,

Winnie works in Winchester,

Joan lives in Japan.

The twins have moved to Tuscany,

Ronald lives in Rome,

Granny's gone to Germany—

And me? I live at home!

Mom, Dad, Auntie Sue,

Andy, Mandy, Uncle Hugh,

Granny, Grandad, Baby Fred,

Annie, Danny, Nelly 'n' Ned,

Dozens of cousins,

Pete's partner, Pam,

Mary's canary,

A goat called Sam,

Rosanna, Roberta, Rosita, and Ron,

Joanna, Janetta, Juanita, and John,

Quite a few nephews,

Nieces and brothers,

Great-great-uncles,

And one or two others,

My second cousin,

Maurice Magee,

And one more person . . .

Who could it be?

Me!

Just Mom and me,
happily.

Mummy, mummy, sweet as honey,
Busy as a bee,
Buzzing off to earn some money,
Buzzing home to me.

Dads have . . .
Big hands and baseball caps,
Ties and tattoos,
Shoulders to ride on,
Shoes like canoes.
Some dads build houses
But can't make the bed;
This dad is hairy
Except on his head.

My mom says
   Brush your hair,
   Sit still, say "please,"
   Wash your hands,

Your ears, your knees,
   You've left your clothes
All in a heap,
   Don't pick your nose,

Now, go to sleep!

Mommy, Daddy, wake up quick!
My tooth's all wobbly! I'm feeling sick!
    Mommy, Daddy, hey, you two!
Can I come and sleep with you?
    Mommy, Daddy, wake up, please!
The window's open, I'm going to freeze!
    Mommy, Daddy—no, I'm not,
Take off the blanket, it's much too hot!
    Mommy, Daddy, tell the truth,
Ever seen such a wobbly tooth?
    Mommy, Daddy, what d'you think?
Should I go and get a drink?
    Mommy, Daddy, please wake up,
I spilled my drink and broke the cup.
    Mommy, Daddy, I've got an idea,
We could stay awake for the rest of the year!
    Mommy, Daddy, what's that noise?
I heard a burglar, stealing my toys.
    Mommy, Daddy, open your eyes!
My tooth's come out—what a surprise!
    Mommy, Daddy, I'm really unhappy,
I look so silly with my mouth all gappy.
    Mommy, Daddy, wake up fast,
I think I'm going to sleep at last.
    Mommy, Daddy, did you hear what I said?
You nearly pushed me off the bed!
    Mommy, Daddy, turn on the light!
Will the tooth fairy come tonight?
    Mommy, Daddy, wake up soon!
Is there really a man in the moon?
    Mommy, Daddy, one last thing,
When do the birds begin to sing?
    Mommy, Daddy, don't try to hide,
Can't you see it's light outside?
    Mommy, Daddy, stop that yawning!
You can't be tired, it's the middle of the morning!

Sisters squeak and sisters shriek,
Slam the door, refuse to speak.
Sisters sneak and sisters peek,
  Then turn all soft
        and kiss your cheek.

I'm the middle sister,
I think it's really mean,
I'm squashed in between,
Like a canned sardine.
I'm the filling in the sandwich,
That's what I am—
Mom says I'm sweet,
So perhaps I'm the jam.

This afternoon I told my mother,
"I've changed my mind about my brother,
I'd rather have that model plane,
Will you send him back again?"

My brother is bad with bananas,

My sister's not happy with ham,

Neither is keen on tangerines

Or juice or jelly or jam.

My brother's not wild about walnuts,

My sister is choosy with cheese

And carrots and cabbage and custard

And potatoes and pudding and peas.

My brother and sister are fussy,

My brother and sister are rude.

There's only one thing *I'm* not keen on—

I'm not very keen on my food!

It's **NOISY** in this family,
Why does everybody **SHOUT**
And **LAUGH** and **YELL**
And **SLAM THE DOOR**
Whenever they go out?

My sister has a **STEREO,**
My brother likes to **SING,**
The baby **BANGS A SAUCEPAN,**
Then the phone starts to **RING.**

Dad says, "You need a bedroom,
Where you can quietly play,
I'll go and get my **POWER TOOLS**
And

START
WORK
RIGHT
AWAY!"

My brother got lost in the city,
My brother got lost in the crowd.
Although the city was noisy,
My brother was ten times as loud.

Grannies and Grandads

My granny has . . .

Two old dogs

A pile of logs

Shelves of books

Some fishing hooks

Aching feet

A special treat

Jars and tins

Needles and pins

A walking stick

Clocks that tick

A favorite chair

Time to spare

In the woods with Grandad,
Through the winter snow—
One of us is fast,
One of us is slow.

In the woods with Grandad,
Walking on our own—
Grandad keeps on smiling.
"My, how much you've grown!"

In the woods with Grandad,
The sun goes down like gold—
One of us is young,
One of us is old.

Families are like the weather,

Breezy, sunny, warm.

When my two brothers get together

It's like a thunderstorm.

BIG STORM
little brother

BIG HUG
love each other

Some families never stop fighting,
They fight over TV and meals.
Whenever they take a journey,
It's an argument on wheels.

Some days are good,
Some days are bad,
Some days are neither,
Only so-so.
Some days we're sad,
Some days we're glad,
Ups,
    downs,
It's like a family yo-yo.

Family Trees

Rock-a-bye, Grandad, taking a look
At the family photo book,
Dreaming of people he used to know,
A family tree begins to grow.

Newborn babies, plump as fruit,
Great-great-granny at the root,
Brothers, sisters, all together,
On branches that reach out forever.

When you're tiny, like a seed,
Your family is all you need.
It's like a forest gathered round
An acorn growing on the ground.

Look, Mom drives a taxi!

Look, Dad drives a bus!

Look, they're coming home now to

Look after us!

Skirts and shirts and dressing gowns—

The wind begins to blow—

They're like a family upside down,

Dancing in a row!

Wash

Work

Worry

Heave

Haul

Hurry

Run

Rinse

Rub

Skate

Scurry

Scrub

Fuss

Feed

Fight

Buy

Bathe

Bite

Shop

Shave

Shake

Choose

Chatter

Chop

Peep

Paint

Play

Sweep

Sing

Sleep

Daddy at the seaside,

Daddy in the sun,

Daddy on a surfboard,

Daddy having fun.

Daddy getting buried

In sand up to his chin—

"HELP!" he yells.

"Please dig me out

Before the tide comes in!"

Dear Granny,
Matthew's got the measles,
Mandy's got the mumps,
The sea is full of jellyfish,
My bed has got big lumps,
Mommy's got a migraine,
The dog's got a disease,
The car's got a flat,
And we've all got fleas.
This week has been the coldest
And the wettest of the year.
I think the tent is leaking.

P.S. Wish you were here.

To My Granny
Sunny Cottage
Sleepy Drive
Backhomesville

Zooming down the motorway
Or up in a balloon,
On horses, bikes, and rocket ships,
Whizzing round the moon,
On roller skates and racing cars
And speeding subway trains,
Helicopters, hovercrafts,
And supersonic planes,
On submarines and sailing boats,
Cutting through the foam,
Where are we rushing to?
We're all rushing home!

Christmas and birthdays
And Thanksgiving Day,
For picnics and outings,
To talk and to play,
When someone has died
And people feel sad,
When a baby is born
And people feel glad.
At weddings, bar mitzvahs,
The end of each year,
To eat and to dance,
To sing and to cheer.

Look around,
You'll see it's true,
The *world* can get together too—
Sisters and brothers,

Fathers

And

Mothers,

I

Love

You.